DR. HARRY EMERSON FOSDICK'S BOOK:
"THE MODERN USE OF THE BIBLE"
A REVIEW

Dr. Harry Emerson Fosdick's Book: "The Modern Use of the Bible"

A REVIEW

BY

I. M. HALDEMAN, **D.D.**

Pastor, First Baptist Church, New York

———

PHILADELPHIA

THE SUNDAY SCHOOL TIMES COMPANY

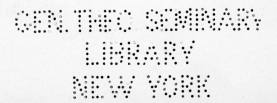

Copyright, 1925, by
The Sunday School Times Company

Printed in the United States of America

TO MY BELOVED SON

HAROLD

*Whose promising life, not only as a
Christian, but as a scientist, was
cut off in the freshness of his years.
In his last and cherished letter he
wrote me these words: "I am a firm
believer. I accept a whole Bible."*

"THE MODERN USE OF THE BIBLE"

The book, "The Modern Use of the Bible," is a collection of lectures delivered by Dr. Harry Emerson Fosdick before the Divinity School of Yale University.

Its thesis is presented with all the mode of final authority, the unmistakable accent of "agreed scholarship," and the emphasis of a conclusion from which, it should seem, there could be no appeal.

Dr. Fosdick analyzes the Bible with absolute assurance.

He speaks with unhesitating frankness concerning its origin.

Origin of the Bible Immature and Childlike

Instead of coming direct from God and bearing the unmistakable stamp of the divine mind, the Bible originated in primitive and childlike ideas.

On page 11 he says:

"A new approach to the Bible has been forced upon us. No longer can we think of the Book as on a level, no longer read its maturer messages back into its earlier sources. We know now that every idea in the Bible started from primitive and childlike origins."

7

Miracles Incredible

The miracles of the Bible are incredible, the modern mind will not accept them.

Citing a list of miracles which he affirms contradict modern astronomy, modern biology, modern physics and modern medicine, Dr. Fosdick tells us:

"They (educated men) find it hard to use one set of mental presuppositions and categories in every other realm of life and another set in religion. They have to shift their mental gear too suddenly when they turn from their ordinary intellectual processes to the strange ways of thinking that the Bible contains" (p. 35).

The God of the Old Testament Shocks the Modern Mind

To Dr. Fosdick the God of the Old Testament is not the God who "inhabiteth eternity," he is a local, limited and tribal God, set up on the plane of surrounding nations.

This God is pictured to us as a cruel and bloodthirsty God, no higher in his moral sense than the people whose crude and racial imagination invented him.

A proof is cited in the "ruthless extermination of the Amalekites—'both man and woman, infant and suckling,' " commanded by this God; and while recognizing the shock it produces to modern sensibility and the indignation it must arouse, at the same time, Dr. Fosdick becomes conservative toward it in endeavoring to define it, not so much as an act of downright inhumanity when judged by moral standards, as the limitation of a tribal God confined by his genesis within a limited field of action.

He draws further attention to the low plane on the part of this God, who as he says:

"Out of pure caprice, at a wayside inn started to kill a man on sight and was only estopped by the quick action of the man's wife in circumcizing her son" (p. 15).

Such a God he is sure "was not a God with whom close communion would be desirable."

The unequal impulses and unbalanced sense of right and wrong in the Old Testament are clearly demonstrated, he thinks, in that this God "equally hates David's sin with Bathsheba and David's taking of a census" (p. 23).

It was only, we are told, as the prophets got away from this primitive, national and tribal idea of God that they "widened their sense of moral obligation."

To have held on to this Bible idea of God (the inference is a fair one) would have made them as immoral as the immoral Bible God himself.

The Text of the Bible a Framework of Shifting Human Experience

When we turn to an examination of the Old Testament construction we find it as stratified as the earth itself.

Each era in which the distinctive parts were written bring evidential witness to the growth of the human mind, its steady emergence from immaturity, the loosening of the shackles of superstition, ignorance and tradition, a larger moral concept, a more sane, a better and kindlier vision of God.

"The framework" (a word used throughout the book to indicate the text) through which the ideas of the Bible proceed has the color, the strength and weakness of its times, is not to be taken seriously, that is to say, not authoritatively, and is to be tolerated only in so far as it gives passage to soul experience.

The experience may be expressed in forms

which in themselves are untrue in fact, contradicted both by science and history, but in so far as the experiences are true, real, soul experiences, there need be no quarrel with them.

Science and history may say, "these forms, these assignments of cause cannot be defended, but the experiences they so faultily endeavor to express are true. The miracle may be rejected as obviously without foundation, we need not bother to believe it at all, but we may accept without restraint a human experience which through all the blunder and crudity, actual superstition and, even, downright falsehood, seeks to prove the soul's reach after truth."

It is here we have the substance of Dr. Fosdick's book and the principle upon which it is written.

From the beginning (it is the suggestion he gives us) there has been an ethical urge in man. You may, if you like, call this ethical force or tendency a deposit of divinity, an elemental manifestation of God in humanity. This ethical impulse has been moving man upward toward spiritual apprehension of, and an intensive desire to serve, God.

It has expressed itself in this book we call the Bible.

Always the experiences have been essentially true, the forms through which they passed have been temporary, finding their character in the times out of which they were evolved. In giving emphasis to this inner sentiment, statements have been made that are scientifically false and historically untrue.

We have an example of this in the belief about demons.

To modern thought there are no such things as demons. They do not exist. They never did exist, but men used the idea of demons, of evil spirits, to account for the hindrances they found every day in their spiritual quest. These hindrances are just as true now as then. Every man who seeks to climb up spiritually knows them— but they are not demons, and every modern man knows they are not; they are simply the reactions that go with the basic animal constitution of man. We can afford therefore to dismiss belief in demons, but the spiritual and personal experiences are true and we may discern them underneath the superstition and ignorance that invents demons and spirits to explain the conflict.

We are to deal with miracles, with historically false elements in the Bible, in the same way.

They were the best means to express either the causation of evil or the inspiration for and encouragement of the good.

When we repudiate all this temporary form of the Bible, thus demonstrate and prove that these portions of the Bible are not inspired, we do not (Dr. Fosdick says we do not) destroy the Bible; on the contrary (Dr. Fosdick says so), we more fully establish it. We emphasize its authority (to the modern mind, the mind that rejects miracles) because under all may be seen the abiding truth of experience, and this experience with all its tergiversation and crudity and at times utter absurdity, this persistent ethic urge ever ascending, finds its culmination in Christ.

In Him the God who little by little has been revealing himself in man, manifesting himself even in the scientific fables and historical misrepresentations, this God is found in Christ as the expression and proof of the evolution of God in man, in all the sweep and surge of supreme spiritual consciousness.

It is for us in this day to take the life of Christ as he lived it, sun ourselves in the quickening warmth of it, absorb his principles and precepts, follow his ideals and rejoice in a book so true, in spite of all its errors and false concepts both of God and man; so true that as we read it, learn to distinguish between the true and the false in its content, surrender to the living spiritual force in it, we shall find ourselves conscious that we are in Christ and Christ is in us.

Repudiating this "framework" of the Bible, its mere form and phrase, we may be delivered from any necessity of coming to grips with either science or history; and when the scientist would come and with rude hand take this Bible away from us, we may say:

"Stand aside, we have no conflict with you at all. Your objections, if you insist on them, are childish; this Bible is not built on mere form, on rigid collocation of terms, on narrow and useless literalisms, but on the great truth that man has been steadily approaching to what Christ is, to what Christ shows man may attain. We take this Book at its true value as a progressive revelation both of God and man, find it more and more authoritative to our inner sense in proportion as we reject the outer and temporary shell; in proportion as we refuse to be bound by its static thought forms and yield to its spiritual call."

"What is permanent in Christianity (we are told) is not mental frameworks but abiding experiences that phrase and rephrase themselves in successive generations' ways of thinking" (p. 103).

And this, as Dr. Fosdick presents it, teaches the struggle of the divine element in the soul, but at the same time throws the Bible in its written form into an unqualified discard as neither textually inspired nor authoritatively infallible.

While you are rejoicing in this beautiful and heroic struggle of the soul and are moved with admiration at the wonderful way in which the Bible is supposed to record it; while you are apparently gaining everything for humanity, you are losing your Bible as you have been accustomed to read and revere it. You are getting an altogether new Bible—so far as the Old Testament is to be considered, a Bible none of the Apostles of Christ knew, and it may be said, Scriptures Jesus Christ himself (if we are to believe the speech recorded of him) never knew.

And this is the result Dr. Fosdick is seeking to achieve.

He is seeking to give us a new Bible.

A Twentieth Century Bible.

For the Bible handed down to us by the triumphant spiritual faith of our fathers, a faith that believed in the full and textual authority of the Book, he would substitute this modern Bible which his genius and enthusiasm evoke.

The New Testament is built in the same detachable and movable framework as the Old.

It is acceptable in form only as it gives procedure to experiences that can be verified in the soul.

It matters little how many incredible miracle narratives may crowd its pages, and Dr. Fosdick announces they are there, and he does not believe them, he says: "I find some of the miracle-narratives of Scripture historically incredible" (p. 164), —it matters little that these incredible miracle narratives are there; the test must be neither scientific nor historical, it must be the inner test of the soul; in short the value of the record depends entirely upon the response of consciousness in the soul.

When the superstructure of miracles is set aside, when statements utterly and hopelessly unverifiable in scientific and historic content are rejected, we may be thankful the psychic fact remains. The coat may, indeed, be shoddy, but the body underneath remains, and that is the essential thing, that is the real value.

It may be quite easy to unravel the text and show its contradictions, but as the soul's upreach is made bare to the gaze, we need not be troubled that the text itself cannot abide.

The Gospel Narratives Largely Pure Fiction

Dr. Fosdick believes the Gospel records, specially in their miracle statement and personal exaggerations, may be explained by the operation of a principle he defines as "heightening," as "addition."

His proposition is that the nearer we get to first-hand documentary sources the fewer miracles there are, the farther we get away from these sources and get into tradition and report, the more the miracles multiply, become more elaborate and startling.

As an illustration he cites the case of Xavier.

In Xavier's letters and the first-hand accounts of him by his companions, no miracles are ascribed to him; but, when his biographies are written, the pages are literally filled with miracles, and miracles of the most amazing and complex sort.

Dr. Fosdick applies this by calling our attention to certain specified statements in the Gospels.

In Mark (assumed to be the earliest of the Gospels) there are no "birth stories"; that is to say, nothing whatever about the virgin birth.

You get this in Matthew and Luke in full detail.

In Mark, only Jesus walks on the water.

In Matthew, Peter tries it, too.

In Mark, a fig tree denounced in the evening is wilted the next morning.

In the later record the fig tree is cursed in the morning and immediately withers.

Mark records no other marvels at the crucifixion than the rending of the temple veil.

Matthew adds—the resurrection of many bodies of the saints that had fallen asleep.

In Mark, at Gadara, Jesus heals one demoniac.

In Matthew he heals two.

Dr. Fosdick says:

"When we compare Mark and Luke we get the same impression of heightened effect and added detail.   In Luke, though not in Mark, are the stories of the virgin birth and of the angelic apparition to the shepherds.   In Mark, where 'one of them that stood by drew his sword, and smote the servant of the high priest, and struck off his ear,' no miracle is recorded. In Luke, however, the ear is restored—the only example in Scripture of the restoration of an amputated member."

"Luke is especially rich in dramatic additions to the narrative."

"In Mark the story of the descending dove at Jesus' baptism is easily interpreted as a "symbolical description of a spiritual experience, Luke makes the event indubitably physical—'in a bodily form, as a dove'" (pp. 147-8).

When we turn from the Synoptic Gospels and compare them with the later Gospel of John we are face to face with this "heightening of the miraculous element."

In John alone you have turning of water into wine, curing of a man born blind, raising of Lazarus from the dead after he had been four days entombed.

We are exhorted to consider such facts as this, "increasingly well known to thoughtful minds," and find it evident that "we would better come to serious grips with the problem that is here presented."

We are reminded that, "In the Old Testament as well as in the New appears this same tendency to heighten marvels as one retreats from first-hand documents."

In plain language, "heightening for effect," and "added detail," signify that over-zealous disciples, enthusiastic biographers, like those of Xavier, wishing to exalt the name and fame of their Master, invented these amplifications, these details, and thus turned the Gospels into a manufactured fabric largely made out of the whole cloth.

If, therefore, we are staggered, if our scientific sense, our modern mind, should balk at a miracle such as water turned to wine by fiat, or the raising of Lazarus four days dead, we need only to apply the principle of "heightening," of "addition," and, seeing in the stories the manifest evidence of invention, feel ourselves at liberty to reject them, not only as unscientific, without historic evidence, but as the content of falsified records, as unwarranted fiction.

By this method it is evident we may easily get rid of some of the sayings of Jesus, sayings that are hard to reconcile with the proposition that he was merely a man, stupendous sayings in which he flatly affirms pre-existence and co-equality with God, claims such as only a fool or a madman could make if he were, indeed, no more than a naturally begotten and born man.

Admit the "heightening for effect," the "addition of detail," admit that these sayings were put into his mouth by exuberant, but unwise, disciples, and you are relieved from bearing in your mind unbelievable things, and at the same time deliver our Lord from carrying a lot of baggage that impedes, rather than impels, the movement of his story.

On this basis of "heightening," and "addition," invention, fiction, unqualified falsehood and thoroughly immoral construction, we may go back and listen to Jesus, as has been suggested, "over the head of his reporters."

That is to say, listen to the Jesus whom our modern mind may conceive.

That is to say, further:

Whenever Jesus makes a claim or assertion which invalidates or contradicts the testimony of the modern mind concerning him and thus puts him in conflict with science and history, we are at full liberty to affirm he never made any such claim, he never made any such assertion, the language is not his, it is the language of his altogether unreliable reporters, his disciples, his untrustworthy biographers.

On this principle of "heightening," of "addition," we may safely assure ourselves that the miracles accredited to him he never performed, the measureless claims quoted as his he never made.

What a perfect weapon this puts into the hand of the larger minded modernist who finds himself forced to deal with that fundamentalist type of Christian who seeks to defend our Lord's name and reputation by bringing forward the testimony of his miracles and personal claims! No matter how eloquent a Fundamentalist may wax over these evidences that Jesus was more than man, that he was very God, piling up literalism after literalism, actual quotations of Scripture, crushing arguments, as he supposes, against all opponents, leaving them actually nothing to say; all the man who believes in the modern use of the Bible has to do is to restrain his own spirit, and quietly and calmly answer:

"My good friend, I admire your sincerity, but it is based altogether upon a lack of advanced knowledge. I am under bonds to tell you that all this evidence you bring in behalf of the Jesus of the Gospels is entirely worthless, the miracles reported as his he never performed, and all those terrific, irresponsible claims to deity he never imagined, much less made; they have been 'heightened for effect' and 'added' for detail. I am sorry to spoil your oration, but truth and accurate knowledge demand that I speak."

What can a man do in face of that, a man who all along has believed in the integrity of the record? What can he do but heave a sigh, become quiescent and wholly surrendered before this "advanced" knowledge, and in the presence of these genii of modernism, "heightening for effect," and "addition" of detail, watch the figure of the Jesus whom he sought to defend fade away into thinnest mist and finally disappear into the realm of a baseless fiction?

On this principle of "heightening," and "addition," we get the story of Bethlehem's star.

It is intimated that the cosmology of the earlier centuries was inextricably mixed up with astrology, and the disciples under this pervasion of influence and desiring greatly to enhance the wonder of the natal night found it easy "to heighten for effect," and "added" this brilliant detail.

Dr. Fosdick has no place for "birth stories."

He does not openly deny the virgin birth in this book, but he has put himself on record concerning it as a useless biological miracle. It can be accounted for as a story only on the ground of this "heightening for effect," this "addition" for detail.

Dr. Fosdick's Definition of "Vicarious" in the Sacrifice of Christ

Dr. Fosdick believes in the vicarious sacrifice of Christ.

But he believes in it, not in the way the New Testament textually teaches it: that is to say, Christ as a sin-bearer, a substitute, "made sin for us," enduring death as a penalty for sin.

He does not believe the death of Christ had any such character as that.

He believes in vicarious sacrifice as illustrated in the act of David Livingstone, who expatriated himself and gave himself up in whole-hearted surrender to the savages of Darkest Africa that he might bring a blessing to their unillumined souls; the act of self-effacement that led Father Damien to cast his lot amid the helpless lepers, share their foul disease, their suffering and the horrors of their death; the principle of self-denial that led

Florence Nightingale to forego all the comfort, the ease and security of home that, amid the horrors of the battlefield she might minister to the wounded and the dying.

You will look in vain through "The Modern Use of the Bible," to find any suggestion that our Lord came into the world to fulfil the typical sacrifices of the Old Testament, or such direct prophecies as the Fifty-third chapter of Isaiah, where he is represented as a lamb to slaughter led, as an ordained substitute bearing the iniquity and penal suffering judicially due to others.

Nowhere is there a shadow of a hint that he "bare our sins in his own body on the tree"; or, that the blood of Christ "cleanseth us from all sin"; nor the dynamic declaration that we are "sanctified through the offering of the body of Jesus Christ once for all"; and that "by one offering he hath perfected for ever them that are (thus) sanctified"; no quotation of Paul's immense statement of the motive that led to the incarnation of Christ, the great objective purpose for which he came into the world, that clean, clear-cut statement of Paul in Hebrews 2 : 9 :

"We see Jesus, who was made a little lower than the angels for the suffering of death . . .

that he by the grace of God should taste death for
every man."

Vicarious suffering, the vicarious suffering of
Christ on the cross, as Dr. Fosdick teaches it, as
his book proposes it, must not be considered outside the category of the Livingstones, the Father
Damiens and the Florence Nightingales.

Dr. Fosdick Does Not Believe
Christ Rose from the Dead

He says so plainly.

"I do not believe in the resurrection of the
flesh" (p. 98).

The Scripture record declares Jesus rose in the
flesh, so actually in the flesh that he commanded
his disciples to handle him and see that he was not
a spirit, a mere ghost, but flesh and bones; so
actually, according to the record, he did what Dr.
Fosdick confesses "puzzles" him,—he took broiled
fish and an honeycomb, "and did eat before them."

Listen to the Lord's own very words in their
full connection:

"Behold my hands and my feet (and why should
he show them his hands, but that they might see
the print where the nails went in; and why did
he show them his feet but that they might see

where the nails were driven crunchingly through?), that it is I myself (just as they had always known him and looked upon him): handle me, and see (surely handling and seeing signify flesh as an objective both to touch and vision); for a spirit hath not flesh and bones, as ye see me **have**." (And what is that, what does that mean if language has any meaning at all? What does it mean, what is it but the straight, authoritative, headquarters statement that he was not a mere spirit, an impalpable ghost, but just as he said, there before them in flesh, very flesh and very bones?)

According to the record, therefore, the resurrection of Christ was a **resurrection of the flesh.**

Since Dr. Fosdick does not believe in the resurrection of the flesh he does not believe Jesus Christ rose in the flesh, and as the New Testament knows no other resurrection of Christ than resurrection in the flesh, then Dr. Fosdick does not believe in the resurrection of Christ according to the New Testament record, the record which says beyond all possibility of dispute that he **did** rise in the flesh.

Dr. Fosdick must stand convicted, therefore, by

his own words and this record of the New Testament as denying the resurrection of Christ.

Since he does not believe in the resurrection of the flesh both in respect to Christ and to the believer in Christ, he does not believe in the literal resurrection of the Christian dead.

It is true, Paul believed in the resurrection of the flesh, both the resurrection of Christ and the resurrection of the Christian.

He sets forth his belief in that great chapter, the fifteenth of the first epistle to the Corinthians.

Paul believed our Lord rose from the dead in the body in which he died.

He says, not only that Christ died, but that he was buried; thus drawing our attention to that which was dead—the body, and the body alone, and therefore that which alone could be raised up again and made alive.

His body we are told in the Gospel was in the grave till the third day, and it was the open tomb and the absence of the body that appealed to the disciples, and carried to them the evidence of resurrection.

Paul says after our Lord was buried: He rose again.

What relation can the emphasis on burial have

but the intensive emphasis that it was the body which rose from the dead, rose from the place of burial?

If Paul does not mean he rose in the body to which he draws this particular attention that it was buried, then Paul is guilty of playing with words and connection of words to deceive.

But Paul is not trying to deceive.

He means absolutely that Jesus Christ rose in the body that had been nailed to the cross, and by that resurrection robbed death of its power and the grave of its prey.

Indeed, the Apostle makes the bodily resurrection of Christ overwhelmingly important.

He says if Christ did not rise preaching is vain.

Deny the bodily resurrection of Christ and you make the preaching of Christ of no more value than empty sound, of no more value than shifting sand and blowing winds.

This Fifteenth Chapter that has been as a Gibraltar of evidence to the Church of Christ in the past, the rock-ribbed testimony upon which many stand today, look at the silent faces of their dead, and across their tears get the light that shines out of his empty tomb, the light that breaks across those tears as though they were a prism, and turns the anguish of despair into the radiant arch of hope till it spans the grave, that monumental chapter of Apostolic faith has no meaning to Dr. Fosdick, it can have no meaning to the students for the ministry who accept his lectures, and can have no meaning to those who would make his "The Modern Use of the Bible" a textbook, and may, according to Dr. Fosdick's logic, be cut out of the Epistle without damage to the New Testament.

To Dr. Fosdick, immortality is not identified with the resurrection of the body. That idea, however it might be worked out from the Hebrew premise about the body was, finally, due to the influence of Zoroastrianism during the exile.

"During the Exile Zoroastrianism became the mold into which the Hebrew expectations of life beyond death were run" (p. 100).

He then adds:

"A great deal of water has flowed under the bridge since the days when those first disciples thought of life everlasting in Zoroastrian terms. Historically the major agency in crowding out the older ways of thinking has been the Greek philosophy. Its basic premise was the evil of the physical body and the desirability of the soul's escape from its fleshly imprisonment to the realm of eternal spirit. It did not want a bodily resurrection; it wanted to escape from the body altogether" (p. 101).

He quotes Origen as one of the long succession of Christians who, "believing earnestly in immortality, have not associated it with the resurrection of the flesh."

Dr. Fosdick does not believe in immortality as related to the flesh. He identifies immortality with everlasting life. In preaching everlasting life—the continuance of the soul or spirit—he assumes he is preaching immortality.

The truth is "immortality" and "everlasting life" are distinct things.

Everlasting life according to Scripture is a specific gift of the grace of God to those who accept Jesus Christ as crucified Saviour and risen Redeemer, and includes continued existence (that which belongs to all souls) ; but immortality in the Scripture use of the word signifies, always, and only, a deathless, incorruptible body (a blessing and benediction provided for the Christian believer alone).

Immortality to Dr. Fosdick is nothing more than continued existence of the soul; it is the logic of his disbelief in the resurrection of the flesh, and is therefore the state and condition of immortality which he now applies to our Lord.

Since Dr. Fosdick does not believe in the bodily resurrection of Christ he has nothing more to say about it than that it "puzzles" him.

He says:

"We may not know what to make of narratives about his eating fish after his resurrection, passing through closed doors, and offering his hands and feet to the inquiring touch of Thomas" (p. 164).

He questions how far that record is due to the "Hebrew necessity of associating continued life with a physical resurrection."

Then he quotes from a psychic investigator as on a "truer track" than that revealed in the Gospel record and deduces the possibility of a psychic resurrection which, if we keep strictly to philological necessity, is that grotesque, philological contradiction in terms—mere soul resurrection.

But he has nothing to say about the effect of the reported bodily resurrection of Christ.

There is no attempted explanation of the indisputable fact that from the hour of this alleged resurrection the disciples, who forsook the Lord when he was arrested, fled in a whirlwind of cowardly panic and stood at last, shivering and pitifully helpless in the crowd that witnessed and enjoyed the agony of his lingering death—there is no reference to the sudden transfiguring effect this story of the resurrection had on these same disciples.

There is no explanation of the dynamically demonstrable fact that coincidentally with the proclamation of this physical resurrection, these crushed, cowed, vanquished and terror-stricken disciples went forth with the courage of lions, grew eloquent with an eloquence which never before had so anointed human lips and inspired the human tongue, counted it a distinguished honor to endure affliction and to die for him whom they believed had triumphed over death and the grave; went forth to suffer and to die, persisting with their latest breath and in their last agony that they were eye-witnesses and that this record which "puzzles" the man of modern mind was true, and true in all its details.

But even though he denies the resurrection of Christ, Dr. Fosdick believes He is alive.

He says:

"We believe that he is not dead but is risen; that we have a living Lord."

On what ground does Dr. Fosdick believe that?

Will he say he believes it because he feels the life of Christ in him?

That is personal, experimental knowledge—perhaps.

But a Mahometan might say that of Mahomet if he sought to prove he was alive.

A follower of Mrs. Eddy might say that of the inventor of Christian Science.

Experimental evidence is good, but it is good only as it is corroborative of direct evidence.

The disciples did not hand out their experimental evidence to the world, they gave direct evidence. They gave the evidence of eyesight. They gave historic fact.

But where is this Christ whom Dr. Fosdick is sure is alive?

He confesses he knows nothing about the future life.

He says:

"Personally, I do not pretend to know the details of the future life" (p. 102).

Future life begins after death. He has no actual

knowledge then of what takes place after death. He has therefore no actual knowledge about Christ since He died,—no actual, direct, evidential knowledge of Christ whatever.

All he really knows according to his own testimony is that **Christ's body of flesh never rose from the dead** and therefore according to the law obtaining in a physical body **it corrupted** and turned to dust.

And this conclusion that is inevitable from the premise of the non-resurrection of the body **is in direct contradiction to, and is contradicted by, the anticipative declaration and assurance of our Lord speaking through the mouth of the Psalmist; as it is written:**

"Thou wilt not leave my soul in hell (in Hades, the underworld of the disembodied dead) ; **neither wilt thou suffer thine Holy One to see corruption.**"

That in speaking of "corruption," the pre-existent Lord is referring to his body, **his flesh after death,** is demonstrated by the comment of the Holy Spirit speaking through the lips of the Apostle Peter on the day of Pentecost.

The Apostle says:

"**He** (David who wrote the Sixteenth **Psalm)**

seeing this before spake of the resurrection of Christ, that his soul was not left in hell (Hades), **neither his flesh did see corruption**" (Acts 2:31).

Dr. Fosdick Has Nothing to Say of the Priesthood of Christ

It is a striking fact that Dr. Fosdick has **nothing** to say about the priesthood of Christ. Not once does he speak of him as a priest. He ignores that splendid phrase of Paul in the eighth chapter of the Hebrews:

"Now of the things which we have spoken this is the sum: We have such an high priest, who is set on the right hand of the throne of the Majesty in the heavens."

He never says a word of the wonderful way in which Paul compares the efficiency of the priesthood of Christ with the inefficiency of the priesthood of Aaron on the day of Atonement. On that day when Aaron went within the veil, into the Holy of Holies, he could not sit down. He must stand. He could remain only long enough to sprinkle the blood upon the Mercy Seat, and must hasten out lest he die; but Paul tells us, Christ entered into Heaven with his own blood and sat **down** on the very throne of God, and now abides there as the ever-living, interceding priest for his people.

Dr. Fosdick never quotes this assurance and exhortation of Paul:

"Having therefore, brethren (he is writing to Hebrew Christians), boldness to enter into the holiest by the blood of Jesus,

"By a new and living way, which he hath consecrated (opened) for us, through the veil, that is to say, his flesh;

"And having an high priest over the house of God (the Church);

"Let us draw near with a true heart in full assurance of faith, having our hearts sprinkled from an evil conscience" (Heb. 10: 19-22).

To Dr. Fosdick, the Epistle to the Hebrews has no meaning.

He has no concept of Christ as a risen, glorified, immortal priest at all.

And this is of absolute logic.

Priesthood is based on sacrificial death, on vicarious, substitutional death, on death that is penal and judicial.

The typical sacrifice to which Paul refers is the sacrifice of the day of Atonement; but Dr. Fosdick does not see the death of Christ as an act of

atonement. He does not know Christ as the Antitype of the Levitical sacrifices. He speaks of
them in relation to Christ and the Cross in a way
that has all the accent of indifferentism and final
repudiation.

He says:

"The Cross of Christ, . . . has been run
into thought-forms associated with old animal
sacrifices" (p. 230).

All the wonder, the glory, the comfort, offered
to the Christian in the thought that in yonder
Heaven is one tempted and tried in all points as
we are, yet proven to be without sin, a splendid
victor, triumphing over all assault, doing so in
our name and in our behalf; who is there as our
Advocate, there to pray for us, to hear our con-
fessions and give absolution for failures by the
way and cleansing for better service; there as our
Representative, always presenting us in the per-
fection and beauty of his own holiness before God
the Father, presenting us as the children of the
Father; there to take our prayers and offer them
to the Father in the virtue of his atoning death;
there as our life and unfailing resource, as our
Forerunner, pledge to God and pledge to us that
some day we shall enter Heaven, be with him,

where he is, and be like him,—of all this Dr. Fosdick says nothing and believes nothing.

And how could he?

How can he know anything of a risen, immortal Christ as high priest when (according to his statement) Christ has ceased to exist in the flesh?

What can you expect other than silence on the part of Dr. Fosdick concerning the priesthood of Christ?

The Christ he portrays is only a fragmentary Christ, a bodiless Christ, a ghost Christ, not the Christ of victory over death and the grave, and whose empty tomb gives a sin-stained, sorrow-smitten world a gleam of hope; not the Christ who has carried an immortal manhood to the throne of the universe and is seated there as the eternal incarnation and visibility of the otherwise unseen God—nay—**the Christ Dr. Fosdick portrays—is not the Christ of the New Testament record.**

Dr. Fosdick Does Not Believe Christ Will Appear a Second Time to This World

The proposition that Christ did not rise in the flesh necessitates the proposition that he will not come again in the flesh.

Dr. Fosdick says he will not.

"I do not believe in the physical return of Jesus" (p. 104).

This denies the statement made by the Lord himself.

"Hereafter shall ye see the Son of man sitting on the right hand of power, and coming in the clouds of heaven" (Matt. 26:64).

This statement of the Lord makes it impossible to turn that Coming into the invisible coming of the Holy Spirit, or into a mere spiritual coming of the Lord himself; the language in all the integrity of honest intention signifies a Son of man in the flesh, coming in the flesh.

This is an issue between Dr. Fosdick and the Lord himself and is a charge the Lord has not told the truth about his Second Coming.

Dr. Fosdick, of course, has no thought of making such a direct charge against the Son of God. The only way, however, in which he can escape the full meaning of his attitude is to take the ground that the Lord never used the words reported of him, they were put in his mouth by the operation of this serviceable principle of "heightening for effect," by this expansive power of "addition."

But over against Dr. Fosdick's plain and open denial of the physical return of our Lord, the denial that he will come again in the flesh, there is this terrible and accusatory statement of the Apostle John, which, when rendered literally, reads as follows:

"Many deceivers are entered into the world, who confess not that Jesus Christ **is coming in the flesh.** This is a **deceiver** and AN ANTI-CHRIST" (2 John 7).

The God of Nature and the God of Love

Dr. Fosdick is full of sharp criticism, not to say indignation, against the barbarism and cruelty of the God of the Old Testament.

In what way, I would ask, will he apologize for the God (transcendental or immanent) who, at least, "permitted" the barbarity, the anguish and woe of the recent earthquake in Japan; the God who, having all power, allows millions to die of pestilence till they learn through piled up holocausts the best hygiene, and other millions to starve with torturing famine in repeated experience through the slow-moving ages till they learn the secrets of successful agriculture, and even then allows mildew and blasting, caterpillar, or

amazingly ingenious, poisonous bug; or when that
is not sufficiently effective in destruction, allows
cloud burst or cyclonic winds to ruin the harvest
of orchard, of vineyard, and of field?

To call this "nature" and leave it at that, may
be scientific, it may be (as it is) historic, but it is
scarcely satisfactory, and certainly does not respond to the so-called upreach which from the
beginning, we are told, has been moving Godward
in man.

Dr. Fosdick believes in a God of love, of mercy
and peace; he believes in a God of life, life flowing out in fulness and health. All this accentuates
itself in the premise that he is not far from every
one of us; that in him we live and move and have
our being; that he is at rest in his world and at
rest in us, the worst as well as the best of us.

How will Dr. Fosdick accredit all this character
to the God of nature?

How will he reconcile a world full of hate with
a God of love?

How will he reconcile a world full of war with
a God of peace?

How will he reconcile a world full of unchang-
ing cruelty with a God of mercy?

How will he reconcile a world crammed, stained

and fever-smitten with sin, sin that finds its fresh initial whenever a child is begotten, whenever a child is conceived, how will he reconcile all this with a God of holiness?

How will he reconcile a world where the sovereign forces are sickness, disease and death, with a God who is the source of life and health and has all power?

Is there any man on earth today (let us say, the average man) who, had he the power, would not exercise it in behalf of suffering humanity?

Is there one who would not dry the tear, give surcease to sorrow, rebuke disease, banish pain and put an end to death?

What shall be said then?

I ask, is it illogical, is it unscientific, to say such a sentiment on the part of the average man would seem to show that he is more compassionate, more full of mercy than the God of nature?

Is it illogical, is it unscientific, to say the failure of the God of nature to respond to this sentiment in the average man is as much a shock to that man as it may be to the sentiment of the man of "modern mind," when he reads the record of a so-called barbarous and tribal God in the pages of the Old Testament?

If the God of nature wrote it, would it be illogical or unexpected to discover some of the characteristics there of a God who hates sin, who will by no means clear the guilty and in the Scripture simply affirms what he carries out in historic experience that those who sin against him, who violate his law, shall be punished even to the third and fourth generation?

If it be true the God of nature never forgives till the penalty is paid, is it astonishing to find the same characteristic underlying the lineaments and operations of the God of the Old Testament?

But where does Dr. Fosdick get his concept of a God of love?

Does he get it from the ethical Christ whose ethical life he exalts?

Well! It is this ethical Christ (so called) who has given us that text translated into every language and read in every land—that text of texts—John 3: 16.

Read it over slowly and take it in.

This is what it says:

"God so loved the world, that he gave his only begotten Son."

Dr. Fosdick knows, as we all know, that the word "gave" here means "delivered up," "sacrificially delivered up," "delivered up for the benefit of others."

He knows what we all know, that Paul uses the same word and tells out the full detail of its meaning in this unforgettable phrase:

"He that spared not his own Son, but delivered him up for us all" (Rom. 8:32).

Wittingly or unwittingly, Dr. Fosdick gets his vision of God as a God of love from that most brutal and barbarous thing in all history—the cross of Christ.

That cross of which Peter speaks and says:

"Him, being delivered by the determinate counsel and foreknowledge of God, ye have taken, and by wicked hands have crucified and slain."

A statement which involves these wicked hands as foreknown and as contained in the determining of the "determinate counsel," a foreordination and determination which, if the modern mind be logical, it must classify as equally barbarous and cruel as any such act accredited to the God of the Old Testament.

Not only was the act of these men foreknown, but foredetermined.

The act of those "wicked" hands and the awful

death those same hands were instrumental in producing were foreordained, predetermined.

That death of the cross which the Son of God declares he was under commandment from the Father to endure.

"Therefore doth my Father love me, because I lay down my life, that I might take it again.

"No man taketh it from me, but I lay it down of myself. I have power to lay it down, and I have power to take it again. This **commandment** have I received from my Father."

It is in view of this fact of ordination, determination and commandment that the Apostle writes that Christ "became **obedient** unto death, even the death of the cross."

That cross which according to the unbroken consensus of the New Testament is the expression of God's merciless wrath against sin.

That cross whereon Paul, claiming to speak by the inspiration of the Holy Ghost, says, God made him "to be sin for us."

But Dr. Fosdick's scheme seeks to find its fulfilment this side of the cross, so far this side of the cross that it does not touch it at all, does not consider it as a factor worth while, even, to mention as such.

It is the life Christ lived on the earth that arouses the enthusiasm of Dr. Fosdick.

It is the living and ethical Christ appealing to the native ethics in man who brings about an achieved and ethical salvation.

In this he is in irreconcilable conflict with Paul.

Paul passes over the ethical, the earthly side of Christ's life and finds his inspiration in the purpose for which Christ became incarnate.

Paul declares the purpose of this incarnation to be sacrificial death.

He says:

He was made, "a little lower than the angels for the suffering of death"; and that he "by the grace of God should taste death for every man" (Heb. 2: 9).

Dr. Fosdick's program of preaching for himself and the students whom he would prepare for the ministry contradicts Paul's program from beginning to end.

Paul determined to know nothing but Christ and him crucified.

Dr. Fosdick determines to know nothing but Christ and him—non-crucified.

Dr. Fosdick preaches that Christ came into the world to live for men.

Paul preaches that Christ came into the world to **die** for men.

Dr. Fosdick preaches the unfolding of a divine life in men.

Paul says the natural man is at enmity with God, is not subject to the law of God and neither indeed can be.

Dr. Fosdick says man is **ever ascending** to the heights where God dwells in Christ.

Paul says he is ever **descending,** and left to himself will depart from God forever.

Dr. Fosdick insists that man has the **nucleus of spiritual** life in him.

Paul says he is **dead** in trespasses and sins.

There is no point or place of compromise between Dr. Fosdick and the Apostle Paul.

If you accept Dr. Fosdick you must reject Paul.

If you accept Paul you must reject Dr. Fosdick.

Dr. Fosdick preaches altogether **another** Gospel than that of Paul.

Paul says if any man preach **any other** Gospel than that he preaches he is to be accursed.

Here are his exact words:

"But though we, or an angel from heaven, preach any other gospel unto you than that which we have preached unto you, let him be **accursed.**

"As we said before, so say I now again, If any man preach any other gospel unto you than that ye have received, let him be accursed" (Gal. 1: 8, 9).

He declares his Gospel is not of man:

"I certify you, brethren, that the gospel which was preached of me is not after man.

"For I neither received it of man, neither was I taught it, but by the revelation of Jesus Christ" (Gal. 1: 11, 12).

The Gospel that stirred the world and set Christianity in the earth was not the Gospel of Dr. Fosdick.

No.

The Gospel that moved the world was the story of "Jesus and the resurrection," the high and exalted affirmation that, he "was delivered for our offences, and was raised again for our justification."

Paul took the statement of Moses, "without shedding of blood is no remission," and joyously declared that in Christ we have "redemption through his blood, the forgiveness of sins, according to the riches of his grace."

To those whose sins were as scarlet and red like crimson, the Apostle John (Our Lord's most intimate disciple of the twelve) triumphantly announced, "The blood of Jesus Christ his Son (God's Son) cleanseth us from all sin."

The hope this Gospel held out to the Church was the Coming of Christ to the world again, coming so that every eye (over there in Palestine) should see him, and those especially who pierced him.

And in saying this John was simply repeating what the pre-existent Christ himself had said through the mouth of the prophet Zechariah:

"They shall look upon me whom they have pierced."

And this was but in anticipation of that hour when standing in the flesh before his judges he said:

"Hereafter shall ye see the Son of man sitting on the right hand of power, and coming in the clouds of heaven" (Matt. 26: 64).

The Christ of Dr. Fosdick who has ceased, so to speak, from the "framework" of the flesh and survives only in his precepts and principles, or in the spirit of them, is not the Christ who on the night after he rose from the dead appeared to his disciples and announced that a spirit did not have flesh and bones as he said he had.

An Ethical and Not a Sacrificial Christ

Nothing is more expressive of Dr. Fosdick's relation to the Christ of God than the utterance he puts in the mouth of those whom he assumes are impatient with the preaching and the worship of a "theological Christ."

This is the utterance:

"Have done with your theological Christ and give us back Jesus the ethical teacher" (p. 245).

That, of course, is saying:

"Away with the Christ whom the New Testament (when not expurgated) declares to be a sin offering, a substitute and sin bearer, suffering the judgment due to others.

"Talk to us no more about the cross of Christ, his sacrificial death.

"Talk to us only of the man who lived and taught, and whose supreme claim to our suffrage lies in the life he lived here.

"Give us his principles of living and neither the agony nor the doctrine of his death.

"Give us the ethical Christ.

"Never again speak to us of the sacrifice of Christ.

"Never again offend our sensibilities with talk about the 'blood of Christ.'

"If you talk about him, talk only of the mortal life he lived here."

And how will Dr. Fosdick reconcile this merely ethical Christ with the Christ set forth in the unforgettable verses with which John opens his Gospel:

"In the beginning was the Word, and the Word was with God, and the Word was God."

The "Word" in these verses is the Greek *Logos*, and this is what Dr. Fosdick, in his lecture on "Jesus the Messiah" (p. 214), has to say of the use of *Logos* by John:

"Logos was not a Jewish category at all. It was the most familiar, popular way of interpreting the divine approach to man which the Hellenistic world outside of Judaism knew. It was in current use in Stoicism, in Alexandrianism, in Platonism. If one were to be understood in philosophy in that day, one would as inevitably think in terms of that category as today one must think in terms of evolution. Hence, when Jesus was preached to Hellenists, the Logos idea was used."

While it is true John uses *Logos* to express the "Word," since he was writing his Gospel in Greek, he was not thinking in any degree in the terms of Hellenistic philosophy, nor endeavoring to make any concession to that concept of God.

John was a Jew, and when he thought of "the beginning," he thought in the terms of the first chapter of Genesis. He thought in the Hebrew terms of God—**Elohim**; he thought particularly in the terms of the twenty-sixth verse of that first chapter:

"And God said, Let us make man in our image."

In this you have a justification and a revelation.

A justification of the plural term in the fact that the Hebrew word and title for God is a plural noun, and a revelation, in the fact that in God-head there is more than one person, revealed in the expression—"Let us make man"; a further revelation that the person who speaks takes the initiative in creation and that he is the person who speaks for, who utters, the Godhead. He who speaks and utters the Godhead is no less than the Word of God. In the second and third chapters we learn that this person speaking, this Word of God, is the Lord God. We learn that it is the Lord God who in co-ordination with, and as the representative of, Godhead, formed man from the dust of the ground and breathed into his nostrils the breath of life; and that it is he who created the heavens and the earth. In short, it is the Lord God by whom all things were created and made.

When, therefore, John said, "In the beginning was the Word, and the Word was with God, and the Word was God," he was thinking of the Lord God.

This Word (this Lord God), John tells us, "was made flesh, and dwelt among us (and we beheld his glory, the glory as of the only begotten of the Father), full of grace and truth."

The plain and simple fact which John sets before us then is that Jesus Christ was no less than the Lord God incarnate.

Logos as John uses it is not a compromise, made to meet the Hellenistic mind, but an opportunity in the use of the Greek word to pour through it the truth of God and the being of Christ anticipated and revealed in Hebrew terms.

In his endeavor to exalt an ethical Christ and at the same time give Him the atmosphere of divinity (not the divinity that creates heaven and earth, but a divinity that shall be a concession to, and proof of, the divinity common to us all), Dr. Fosdick says, "But if Jesus is divine and if divinity hedges us all about like the vital forces which in winter wait underneath the frozen ground until the spring comes, that is a gospel."

To this he adds:

"Then the incarnation in Christ is the prophecy and hope of God's indwelling in every one of us" (p. 271).

(That is, by nature.)

This explains how Dr. Fosdick can so easily quote such passages as that Christ is "the first born among many brethren," and ignoring, or slipping over all standards of exegetical righteousness, give that which belongs exclusively to those who have openly professed a saving faith in Christ, give it and other passages belonging to the same zone, to all men, believer and unbeliever alike.

It is true, Paul tells us, Christ is declared to be the Son of God, but declared, demonstrated, proved to be such by the resurrection from the dead, and by that selective resurrection becomes the first born among many brethren who, like himself, shall be born (and in the same manner) from the womb of death and the grave.

But Dr. Fosdick goes back (in his intent) to the original birth of Christ and seeks to make

that birth the herald of a common sonship of all
men—a natural and universal brotherhood, calling for a common fatherhood of all men.

It is the divinity in all men pre-eminently revealed in Christ that makes his humanity the
guarantee for an eventual and universally redeem-
ed humanity.

A very startling Christ is he, indeed, whom Dr.
Fosdick would present to us.

Think of the initial fact of this Christ.

That shining, wonderful star of his natal night
a possible fiction **and the nativity itself mostly
fiction.**

Will you face the proposition with which Dr.
Fosdick discounts his virgin birth, the proposition
that it would be a useless biological miracle?

Have you thought straight up and down about
the matter on the basis of the narrative record?

If Christ were not virgin born, then, of course,
in the full meaning of the term and the consequence if he were not so born, he was begotten of
a human father, and that father demonstrably not
Joseph, and therefore the mother of Christ once
publicly and solemnly betrothed to him (and this
betrothal counted as sacred and responsible as
marriage) by the law of Jewish betrothal as

guilty (in the eye of law and custom) as a wife who breaks wedlock; a Christ, because born out of actual wedlock, altogether illegitimate, and because begotten of an unknown father, nothing better than a bastard; a Christ who since he had both a human father and a human mother could not have been the essential and only eternally begotten Son of the Father, and therefore no more supernatural than other humanly begotten and born sons of men.

Not only that, but if he were begotten of a human father, as that father was sinful, then he had a sinful nature; having a sinful nature he was under the penalty of death; therefore he did not tell the truth when he said he could lay down his life and take it again at his will; not only that, but as he was under penalty of death for original sin, he needed a Saviour; not only that, he needed to be regenerated.

This is the incontrovertible logic of denying the virgin birth.

Having taken away from Christ the right to be considered the antitype and complete fulfilment of the Hebrew sacrifices; having denied necessarily any atoning value in his death, any redemptive or legally cleansing value in the shedding of his blood; having denied that he rose from the dead, "according to the scriptures," and will never return to this world; having taken away every distinctive lineament of him as the Scriptures present him, Dr. Fosdick tells us he is the final expression of that divinity which is common to us all—and since common to all—the divinity that was in Judas who betrayed him and in the thief who reviled him.

This consummative, ethical Christ is the Christ Dr. Fosdick brings before us, the Christ whom he tells us he loves, the Christ whom he adores, whom he would have us likewise love and serve.

This is Dr. Fosdick's Christ, the Christ he finds in the Bible, but only in the Bible when it is modernly used; only after its thought forms are recognized as shifting and temporary; only after the miraculous and supernatural side of Christ is deleted from its pages, so deleted that any one who has been accustomed to read of him and follow him according to the ancient use of the Scriptures may well cry out with Mary, "They have taken away my Lord, and I know not where they have laid him."

It is the exaltation of this Christ Dr. Fosdick has discovered that startles you, confounds you.

His enthusiasm for this Christ is overflowing, unbounded.

He speaks of him as the abiding figure on the horizon of time. All other figures pale before him as the stars before the sun. He talks of his reproductive power in the lives of men, his living force in human hearts. He talks at times in ways that could not be called less than "orthodox," with all the accent that may be put upon the word. He speaks of a "living" Lord, till the unwary listening to the great exaltation would say, "Dr. Fosdick is one of the most loyal and loving preachers of Christ in the world, he exalts him, glorifies him, wins your sympathy with his sympathy and makes you enthusiastic with his enthusiasm"; but the hard, cold fact is this: the Christ whom Dr. Fosdick so richly and in jeweled phrases preaches is **not the Christ of the New Testament at all.** It is a Christ **evolved out of his inner consciousness and intensive imagination.** It is a Christ he has created and built up for himself, a Christ who does not, and never can, exist save in the imagination of the man or men who rob Him of every right and title that is his, rights and titles that can be taken from him only by tearing to pieces and destroying the Scriptures that record them.

Behold how Dr. Fosdick has robbed him of all the New Testament gives him: he has robbed him of the golden crown of deity and replaced it with the tin foil crown of a divinity common to man. He has robbed him of the right to take his body out of the grave, and having barred the earth against him at every point of the compass, says he shall never come back to this world, that we shall never see him again on this earth.

This is the Christ "The Modern Use of the Bible" would exhort the ministry to preach in our churches, teach in our Sunday-schools and proclaim in foreign lands.

This is the Christ whom, after he has been purged from all that is supernatural, Dr. Fosdick has the courage to call "divine."

This So Called Divinity of Christ is a Divinity Minus Omnipotence

But lest some echo of Nice or Chalcedon should be misinterpreted and the abundant and all-embracing phrase that neither time can alter nor custom stale, even that phrase, "God of God, and very God of very God"; lest that mighty collocation, that piled-up wealth of definition, should lead

some unsuspecting soul to transmute "divinity"
into "deity," and thereby spoil the whole scheme
of which "The Modern Use of the Bible" is the
full expression, Dr. Fosdick pulls down any tempt-
ing structure built upon the device of councils and
the plastic, metaphysical imagination of men, and
definitely defining this ubiquitous word, "divinity," gives us the fixed, even, "static" lineaments
of the divine Christ he would have us believe in
and over whom in uplifted phrase his enthusiasm
flames out.

This is the way in which he defines and determines the divinity of Christ:

"In everything that matters to our spiritual
life, very God came to us in Christ."

That sounds large, full, complete, and has
apparently a horizonless sweep; but then he adds,
and the explicatory addition comes like the crash
of unexpected thunder on the stillness of a cloud-
less sky—these shattering words:

"To be sure, nobody should ever go to Jesus, to
his manger and his Cross, to find the omnipotence
which swings Orion and the Pleiades. Omnipotence
in that sense is not revealed there" (p. 269).

Although Dr. Fosdick tells us not to quibble
about a supposed difference between divinity and

deity that is not really there; although he assures
us this distinction rests upon an endeavor to think
of God in terms of metaphysical substance and
Pure Being conceived apart from spiritual quality,
and that the insistent endeavor to define the relation of Christ with him in the same terms is an
endeavor useless for religion and "properly outlawed from good philosophy," in spite of the theological and academical turn to the clause, the fact
remains that the divinity with whatever of "very
God" may somehow be in it in the "spiritual"
quality with which it environs it and shields itself
is—

Divinity **minus** Omnipotence.

However it may be good or bad philosophy, the
fact as Dr. Fosdick states it cannot be ignored.

This is the fact:

The divinity of Christ is divinity minus omnipotence.

And Dr. Fosdick is able to say this in face of
the unrebuked exclamation and full confession of
Thomas that no amount of ingenuity can modify:

"My Lord and my God."

He says it in face of Paul's direct statement
that Jesus Christ created all things.

Paul leaves us in no doubt about that creative
action.

He says:

"By him were all things created, that are in heaven, and that are in earth, visible and invisible, whether they be thrones, or dominions, or principalities, or powers: all things were created by him, and for him: and he is before all things (therefore, uncreated) and by him all things consist" (are "held together," and this is saying nothing less than that the universe is Christo-centric).

Dr. Fosdick denies omnipotence to Christ in face of that other immense affirmation of Paul:

He "upholdeth all things (and therefore Orion and the Pleiades) by the word of his power."

He denies omnipotence and therefore deity to Christ in face of the doubly reported declaration of God the Father, owning the pre-existent Christ as his Son:

"Thy throne, O God, is for ever and ever."

Dr. Fosdick makes his statement about omnipotence in face of our Lord's own claim as he stood in the reported "flesh and bones" of his resurrection body:

"All power (and what is that but omnipotence?) is given unto me in heaven and in earth."

I have no particular wish to turn this article I am writing into controversial argumentation; to

leave Dr. Fosdick's bare statement alone, to let
it stand out by itself in its absolute nakedness,
ought to be sufficient to classify his definition of
divinity in so far as it relates to God's Christ and
God's Son. But I am under bonds to this opportunity as a witness for the New Testament Christ,
now that the challenge is thrown down, to consider for a space the claims which He made for
himself when on the earth; nor can these claims
get intermittance of essential right whether we
balance the difference between pre-existence and
incarnation or any lapsing space between the two
given points, the manger and the cross; for, if
Christ were ever God at all, God the Son as
well as Son of God, he was as much God with the
attribute of omnipotence, as much God in substance, being and personality, when he was
wrapped in swaddling bands in that body he had
accepted as the "prepared body" from the Father;
as much God, very God, when, indeed, as God he
offered on the cross the humanity he had created
for himself and for that purpose; as much very
God there between those two points, the manger
and the cross, as in any time or eternity of his
personal acting; for, accepting the record that he
was pre-existently in the "form of God," at no

point in eternity did he "empty himself" of more than his form and appearing as God.

Let us hear some of the claims he made for himself in the days, we will say, of "his flesh."

He said whatever the Father did, he himself, as the Son of the Father, could do "likewise"; that is, "same-wise," in the same manner, under the same impulse, or power.

Let us get his full utterance:

"What things soever he (the Father) doeth, these also doeth the Son likewise" (John 5:19).

Since the "wise" in which the Father did things was as Omnipotent God, the "likewise" which Christ claimed as the Son was the claim that he could do things even with the omnipotence of the Father.

To astounded Jews he once said:

"Before Abraham was I am."

They took up stones to stone him.

And why?

Not because he claimed pre-existence,—they had no objection to that,—but because in giving his answer he said:

"I am."

He did not say, "Before Abraham was, I was."

No, he said: "I am."

In saying that, saying it under the circumstances and in the form he did, banishing both past and future as any part of his personal existence, and radiating the idea that he in himself possessed a being that was ever abiding and therefore a changeless present, he actually claimed to be he who at the burning bush defined himself as, "I am that I am."

It was because he linked the sacred and incommunicable name of the sovereign God to his own selfhood that they sought to stone him, to kill him, to put an end to him as a wicked blasphemer, not fit to live.

To equally astonished listeners in the temple he uttered this, if you please, metaphysical statement, this unmitigated and challenging proposition:

"I and my Father are one" (John 10:30).

To be sure it is little more than kindergarten analysis to recognize the numerical adjective as in the neuter and therefore to be assured when he said, "I and my Father are one," he actually said, "I and my Father are one thing."

That certainly was stating a "relation."

As a thing is a substance, then he and the Father would be one in some substance.

In the under meaning of the term therefore the phrase may read:

"I and my Father are one substance."

We are under no necessity to speculate about it, we know the substance of the Father is,

"Pure Being."

Thus Christ actually said:

"I and my Father are one Pure Being.

The Being of the Father we are agreed is deity.

In the meaning of the term our Lord actually said:

"I and my Father are one deity."

Because of the poverty of the richest language, we are forced to translate the word and idea of "deity," by that other word—"God."

The climax of it then is this, in saying "I and my Father are one," our Lord Jesus Christ said:

"I and my Father are one God."

It is not necessary to affirm that either Nice or Chalcedon were in his mind, but I know no reason why they might not have been there; indeed, it would be difficult to see how they were not, owning him as God, as very God. I see no reason why he did not know them as the coming formative centers of a final and justified theology in respect to his personality and being.

It is not necessary I should expand this utterance of Jesus Christ in all its content, which the logic of intensive study and analysis afterward forced men to conclude as in the essence of his being and its relation. It is all there in these simple but majestic words:

"I and my Father are one."

By this utterance he did say:

"My Father is one person to whom I say, 'Thou'; I am another and distinct person to whom my Father says, 'Thou.' Although my Father and I are distinct persons, so that he is the Father and not the Son, and I am the Son and not the Father, yet the Father and I are one undivided and Pure Being—one God."

The modern mind may be unable to receive this definition and upon this basis, the basis of that simple expression, "I and my Father are one."

The excited crowd of Jews ready to mob him, to stone him to death, had no difficulty in reaching a conclusion as to the meaning and intent of the words.

Because they had no difficulty about it they took up the stones to stone him.

When he asked why they would stone him, this is the answer they gave him:

"Because that thou, being a man, **makest thy-self God**" (John 10:33).

They knew he meant both in essence and atti-tude he was very God the Son, as much as the Father was very God the Father.

No greater claim of omnipotence than the claim made in the words of Jesus Christ could be made.

And it is to be repeated, there is no point either at the manger or at the cross where he could be less than what his claim would make him to be— essentially God.

He could **restrain** his omnipotence.

He could do that **because** he **was** omnipotent.

Only God could so restrain his omnipotence.

But—he could not cease to be essentially God at **any point** in his existence; as it is written:

"He cannot **deny himself**" (2 Tim. 2:13).

There is yet another claim:

The claim made in his final prayer in John 17, and in the most amazing part of that amazing prayer:

"And now, O Father, glorify thou me with thine own self with the glory which I had with thee (literally, 'by thy side') before the world was."

There are the recorded claims of Jesus Christ—

claims from which essential relationship cannot be "outlawed."

How shall we deal with them?

They are there.

Something must be done with them.

Shall we do as has been suggested when such literalism confronts us—go back and listen to Christ "over the head of his reporters"?

Shall we charge these reporters with taking the simple, spiritually intended words of Christ as originally uttered, changing their form, "heightening for effect," "adding," actually putting into his mouth words he never uttered, and of which he never dreamed?

Let us get back, however, to Orion and the Pleiades.

If Christ were not virgin born, if he were humanly begotten; if he had only the humanity a human father gave him, then Dr. Fosdick is entirely in the right when he denies him any claim to omnipotence, whether in the manger, on the cross, or at any time between his birth and his death.

No mere man, nay, no exceptional man, in whom there may be a deposit of the divinity common (as it is said) to all men, could by any means swing Orion and the Pleiades.

Here then by the ministration of Dr. Fosdick we have arrived.

We are at the termini.

They are there for us to contemplate:

A Christ without omnipotence.

A Christ subject to the interpretation of modern mind.

A Christ whose history has been largely invented, whose supreme claims are fiction, whose miracles were never performed.

A Bible contradicted by science, unreliable in history, not always moral, and whose shifting thought forms, whose uncertain "framework," make it of avail only as it can be proven by personal experience.

Nothing more destructive to the ancient or former use of the Bible, nothing more nullifying to its former value in the general mind, nothing more challenging to the fact of Christ it has been accustomed to proclaim, has ever been written than this book, "The Modern Use of the Bible"; not the coarse sentences of a Paine, the pretentious logic of a Hume, the slavering foulness of a Voltaire, nor the cheap misrepresentations and

conundrum-like utterances and denunciations of
an oratorical Ingersoll, have ever more deliber-
ately, though subtly and often most attractively,
sought to ruin confidence in the Bible our fathers
loved and whose faith and piety are our heritage.

The Modern Use of the Bible Necessary to Keep the Educated Generation in the Church

In view of all this, therefore, it is legitimate
that I should ask on what ground does Dr. Fosdick as a professed Christian, a minister of the
Gospel of Jesus Christ, and a teacher of students
for the ministry,—on what ground does he justify
himself in repudiating the ancient, and demanding the modern, use of the Bible?

He tells us much, and enthusiastically, about
new evidence (not for, but against the ancient
use of the Bible)—knowledge unfamiliar to men
of former times, new instrumentalities with which
more accurately to determine the value of a text.

But surely he knows that none of this has
affected, nor can in any way affect, the fundamental statements of the Book as to man's constitution, sin, death, the person of Christ, the fact
of his cross, the record of his resurrection, ascen-
sion, and the multiplied statements as to his Sec-

ond Coming. There is no new text that can, even in a degree, change the angle, the setting, nor the intrinsic value of these granite statements.

All the increased knowledge apart from the text of the Bible does not render untenable the great, recorded decree of the Son of God:

"Except a man be born again, he cannot see the kingdom of God."

Dr. Fosdick himself involuntarily testifies that the Babylonian literature out of which at one time it was so categorically stated Moses had drawn the cosmological record of Genesis, has been proven to be a lot of pitiful rubbish and altogether negligible stuff.

The larger and more critical attainment in Greek scholarship has not changed that immense, far ringing, confessional phrase:

ὁ κύριός μου καὶ ὁ θεός μου.

It seems out of place to talk about scholarship as the special endowment or equipment of an oligarchy of candor, a hierarchy of particular sincerity, within whose restrained and special circle the truth will be told and not even the suspicion of obscurantism tolerated; very startling to talk in such fashion in the face of men who bring accredited scholarship and untainted sincerity in their support of the old text and who kneel at the feet of a Christ concerning whom they say as reverently and as fully as did Thomas of old:

"My Lord and my God."

Men who find all the newly discovered readings have not changed a single accent in the sweet clarity of that Gospel which testifies God the Father made his Son who knew no sin to be sin for us, so many of us, who seem to know nothing so much as sin, that we might be made the very righteousness of God in him.

But Dr. Fosdick persists in environing himself in the atmosphere of "advanced," and "agreed," scholarship and by it finds his justification for demanding a modern use of the Bible.

He justifies himself on the ground that as now written and edited, the Bible actually contradicts, and is contradicted, by science, by history and human experience.

Every year, we are told, an army of young men and young women are pouring out through the gateway of school, academy, college and university and, unless something is done to avert the catastrophe, this rising generation, filled with the new knowledge which science brings, unable to accept the Bible as it has been interpreted, will repudiate it, turn their back upon the Church and refuse to listen, even, to its attempted ethics.

To save this generation, these future molders of the world, the Bible must be interpreted in the light of science, on the plane of an enlarged concept of humanity and the possible consciousness of God in the soul.

Better a thousand times (that is the logic of this conclusion)—better a thousand times cut to pieces the Old Testament with its blood-thirsty and exterminating God; better join hands with the scientist in repudiating the unscientific and merciless God it portrays and banish him forever from the consideration of men; better cut out of the New Testament every recorded miracle accredited to Christ, every claim reported to be made by himself; better turn the Gospels into an accepted patch work of fiction and the epistles, particularly those of Paul, inspired by his reaction from the Torah and the complications of the Talmud, into nothing of more value than the expression of personal opinion; better to take the crown of deity from Christ and reshape it into a divinity of "spiritual quality" only; better seal up the tomb and keep within it the dust of his unrisen body; better repeat over and over again that his resurrection is nothing more than the persistence of his precepts and principles; better all that at any cost to the worth of the New Testament and the Bible as a whole, than by an out of date and lamentable perversity hold on to it in the old, absurd and exploded idea that it is the "inspired, inerrant, infallible Word of God," and thus drive this scientific new generation into the undertow of an ever deepening tide of materialism.

In short, to save this generation from a moral and spiritual debacle; in order to save them for God and their fellow men, it is better to cast away this Book than persistently present it as the perfect and final revelation from God to man.

Here, indeed, is the secret of Dr. Fosdick's attitude to the Bible. He would take out of it all that is miraculous, supernatural, and superhuman, **in order that he may make it acceptable to the natural man;** a Bible that may be received by the natural heart of unbelief as readily as a newspaper or a magazine article; and this too, in face of the declaration of Holy Scripture that "the natural man receiveth not the things of the Spirit of God: for they are foolishness unto him: neither can he know them."

Dr. Fosdick Elusive and Contradictory

In spite of his quality as a writer Dr. Fosdick is elusive and to a degree contradictory as a thinker, and is always, by virtue of this endowment, escaping from the point where you would hold him to the logic of his basic propositions.

At one moment his writing is as fully infidelic in form as that of any openly confessed infidel, just as caustic, just as relentlessly destructive, turning ancient faith into folly and modern confidence into absurdity; and then, suddenly, he will turn and appeal for a more intensive faith in the Book which he has endeavored to break and mutilate; or, exalting it to a plane where he demonstrates the poverty and intellectual ruin that would fall on the world were the world robbed of it, he will immediately snatch it from you as a fetish and rebuke your devotion to it as a bibliolatry of which you should be ashamed. At one moment giving you a stab of criticism, in which the criticism is so double-edged with scientific assertion and the cold steel of cynicism that every nerve of faith and hope in respect to the Book is paralyzed, he will turn again and as with a royal largess pour into your heart the all-pervading

balm of assurance for every doubt, bidding you
believe what you have lost you have in reality
gained.

As an example of this elusiveness and the
undercurrent of contradiction, note what he has
to say about miracles.

"We do not accept Biblical narratives of the
miraculous as an act of faith. We do it, if we
do it at all, because we are historically convinced.
Approaching the Bible so, there are some narratives of miracles there which I do not believe.
To suppose that a man in order to be a loyal and
devout disciple of our Lord in the twentieth
century A. D. must think that God in the ninth
century B. C. miraculously sent bears to eat up
unruly children or made an axe-head swim seems
to me dangerously ridiculous * * * Joshua making
the sun stand still may be poetry and the story of
Jonah and the great fish may be parable; the
miraculous aspects of the plagues in Egypt and
the magic fall of Jericho's walls may be legendary heightenings of historical events; the amazing tales of Elijah and Elisha may be largely folk-
lore; and, in the New Testament, finding a coin
in a fish's mouth to pay the temple tax, or walk-
ing on water, or blasting a tree with a curse, may

be just such stories as always have been associated with an era of outstanding personalities and creative spiritual power. Certainly, I find some of the miracle-narratives of Scripture historically incredible" (pp. 163, 164).

Having classified these miracles as poetry, or parable, legendary folk-lore, "heightenings," that is, invention, pure fiction, narratives to him utterly incredible, Dr. Fosdick comes back on the basis of psychic research in respect to the "puzzling" record of the resurrection of Christ, as indicated by a psychic investigator whom he quotes, and with an evident desire to tone down the shock his repudiation of the miracles cited might give, says:

"There is no use in pretending that we know more than we do, and about many an ancient miracle-narrative a man may well suspend judgment awaiting light" (p. 165).

Another illustration of this elusive method and the seeming involuntary and contradictory swing back in a rush of rhetorical exaltation of the Book his rationalistic statements have so maltreated (just as though one who had smitten you in the face turned and graciously offered an emollient whose application should take away some of the inflammation produced by the blow), after having frankly stated the origin of the Bible is immature and childlike, he glorifies the opening lines of that Bible in this softening and gracious fashion:

"When one turns from this welter of mythology (Babylonian) to the first chapter of Genesis, with its stately and glorious exordium, 'In the beginning God created the heavens and the earth,' one feels as though he had left miasmic marshes for a high mountain with clean air to breathe and great horizons to look upon" (p. 52).

After calling the Bible a "framework" and its construction mere shifting thought forms whose language is a speech two thousand years out of date, whose "every idea started from primitive and childlike origins," many of whose statements are only fiction, and whose miracle narratives are "incredible," is there anything finer than this from any man's pen or tongue?

Just this:

"As for our English classics, take from them the contribution of the Scriptures and the remainder would resemble a town in Flanders after the big guns were through with it" (p. 3).

It is this elusiveness, this softening the blow before or after it is given, this sudden appeal to

the residuary and reminiscent belief, even, in the
most naturally unbelieving that disarms suspicion
and leads people, some people, really to believe
that Dr. Fosdick is the prophet who is seeking
to clear away all obstacles to faith and is in truth
devoting himself to the defense of the Bible.

His elusiveness becomes vagueness—when dip-
lomatically necessary.

Take the full lecture on miracles.

Did any man ever before use such terms, such
definitions of miracles, such denial of any that
cannot be verified historically, and yet such assurance that miracles are within the law and should
be fully expected today?   And then when we are
on the eve of recognizing God has (because
of his own limitless being, because his own being
is a miracle) all embracing laws out of sight that
may include any operation which seems against
what we have known as law heretofore, we
find suddenly the miracles to which reference is
made are in reality nothing more than providen-
tial guidance of men, God's moral action in men, so
that, by the time we are at the end of the treatise,
we are in an impasse and are forced to conclude
this uninterrupted run of smooth, flowing speech
about miracles is after all only another skillful

use of language to hide the undercurrent of real thought. Surely, I should not wish to be less than courteous, but I am satisfied were a premium offered to the person who could find out what Dr. Fosdick actually means by miracles, no man would ever come forward to claim the prize.

And yet when you allow this outwardly vague utterance to permeate and dissolve in your mind you are persuaded that when Dr. Fosdick says some miracles to him are incredible as reported, he means all recorded as such in the Bible are, finally and flatly, incredible and impossible, to him.

After every thrust at the literal reading of the Book he comes back to spiritual experience and skillfully substitutes experience for the text itself.

It is this constantly attempted exaltation of the spiritual side of the Bible, the spiritual that is said to run through it, experiences that are verified more or less in every age and in every individual history, which blinds the average person who reads a book like "The Modern Use of the Bible," or hears its exalted sentiments in spoken addresses, and takes away for the time being all the effect of the smashing blows given to the verbal integrity of the Bible.

Applauded by Infidels

That in the twentieth century Dr. Fosdick should teach this Bible whose thought forms he believes to have been outgrown and now hopelessly out of date; that he should teach this Bible to be the ceaseless power for producing spiritual experience, and in proportion as we get rid of its thought forms, rebuke the literal interpretation of it, the foolish attempt to find typical characteristics and make them the key and demonstration of supposedly fundamental truths; the more we accuse it and prove it guilty of falsehood in verbal terms; the more we smite and reject its claims as directly inspired of God, in that proportion, we exalt the Bible, recommend it, and help make it the abiding source of spiritual experience; that Dr. Fosdick is willing to do this shows a high state of courage and an intense enthusiasm which, when all verbalism is laid aside, is just pure, cold, measureless unbelief, the unbelief that is of the same quality to be found in every unregenerate mind and accentuated in every unqualified infidel.

And it is a startling revelation of the inner quality of Dr. Fosdick's book, its appeal to the natural unbelief in man and the quick apprehension the natural mind has of its quality, that some of the warmest commendations come from those who have no place for any kind of a Christ, and to whom the Bible has always been and ever will be nothing more than a human product of unequal values, and under no condition and in no sense whatever a revelation from God.

Even those who hate Christ and would destroy the Bible applaud Dr. Fosdick's book; they applaud it because they see in it the entering wedge to destroy faith in the Christ who has been worshiped and adored as God, even when loved and trusted as perfect man.

They see in it the force that would help dislodge the Bible from its place of authority in the mind and soul of man, and open more widely the door of that naturalism which gives no welcome to a transcendental, interfering and finally judging God.

Dr. Fosdick a Dangerous Teacher

I consider Dr. Fosdick the most dangerous teacher in the professing Church, and just because of some of these qualities I have outlined, his elusiveness, his now and then swinging back

with exalted utterance as though he had found a
way by which he could reveal faith in the Bible
and in God's Christ as never before, his apparent
defense of the Bible (what he allows to remain of
it), and his glorification of Christ (after he has
actually robbed him of the glory the Bible would
give him), all this insistent demand for the high-
est type of Christian faith and devotion to Christ,
give him an open door and a quick entrance to
minds not on guard, and specially to that type
of mind which makes charity cover any multitude
of sins, who would think no evil and would accept
honest motive even though it "might pave the way
to hell," and who recognize sincerity as sufficient
grace for any attitude.

All that the worst enemy has ever said against
the Christ of the New Testament as the New Testament stands, in the denial of his miracles, his
claims, his omnipotence, his redeeming blood, his
bodily resurrection, and the blessed, sunlit hope
of his Coming again; all that the most conscience-
less critic has ever said against the verbal integrity of the Bible, he has said; all that could be
given as a demonstration that it is not the fully
inspired, inerrant, infallible Word of God,—the

final, fixed authority for the soul of man,—he has given.

But he does all this while calling the Christ whom he preaches—Master (and no one uses that word "Master" with greater unction), testifying of his devotion, his adoration and boundless desire to glorify him (although it is impossible to visualize him if he did not rise in the flesh, the only vision he can really have of him being the yesterday of his life on earth).

It is this attitude so many see, rather than the emphasis of his destructive criticism which they hear.

It is **this subtle use of orthodox phrases,** while **in his heart of hearts he does not believe in** the **facts those phrases express,** which renders Dr. Fosdick so actually dangerous.

Nothing can more dramatically and dynamically show the utter destructiveness of Dr. Fosdick's teaching in its ultimate overthrow of the Christ of the New Testament, than the scene at Bethany.

I do not mean merely the resurrection of Lazarus, but the words of our Lord to Martha.

He said to her:

"I am the resurrection, and the life: he that

believeth in me, though he were dead, yet shall he
live:

"And whosoever liveth and believeth in me shall
never die."

Now, all the ingenuity in the world cannot get
away from the fact that when he said, "though
he were dead, yet shall he live," he meant a person in general who should be just as dead as
Lazarus then was as to his body in his four-day-
old grave; and that this dead person (dead as
Lazarus was according to the record) should be
made alive in his body, that his body should be
made alive.

There cannot be, there ought not to be, any
doubt that absolute logic requires us to under-
stand the words of our Lord as follows:

"He that believeth in me, though he were dead
(dead in his body), yet shall he live (be made alive
in his body, **when I come**):

"And whosoever liveth (is alive in his body)
and believeth in me shall never die (in his body.
when I come)."

That this exegesis is absolutely sound and is
wholly and entirely impregnable is seen, demonstrated, and proved, in the triumphant announce-
ment of Paul:

"We shall not all sleep (die in our body), but we (believers who are alive in the body) shall all be changed (not die),

"In a moment, in the twinkling of an eye, at the last trump: for the trumpet shall sound, and the dead shall be raised incorruptible, and we (those who are alive) shall be changed."

All this exclusively, of course, in relation to those who are in Christ, and who are Christ's and whose resurrection and transfiguration will take place as Paul tells us, "at his coming."

Here then you have just what Christ said to Martha, not only as a promise whose local fulfilment should be then and there at Bethany, but as a general proposition that when he should come to the world again the dead who had fallen asleep in his name should be raised from the dead as to the body and the living who believed in him should never die.

But, if Christ did not rise in his body, in his flesh (as Dr. Fosdick says he did not); if he cannot and will not come again (as Dr. Fosdick says he will not), then the dead who died in the faith of him will not rise from the grave (as Dr. Fosdick says they will not); nor ever will the time come when Christians shall cease from dying, but like dumb driven cattle that go stumbling to the slaughter, they shall go one after the other, young man and maiden, father, mother, all the tender, linked up relations of life, to the blackest scandal on the face of the earth, the grave of corruption and tongueless silence.

Then the promise made to Martha, and through Martha to the Church,—the promise which was to be literally fulfilled,—as it was fulfilled at Bethany by his Coming, will never be fulfilled.

The Christian minister who believes Dr. Fosdick's teaching dare not quote this Bethany utterance of our Lord. He will be smitten in his own self respect if he do so; for, unless these words are associated with our Lord's second, personal and physical Coming, they have no meaning even in the most intense endeavor to rarify them by spiritualizing them.

When he shall be called to speak a word over the dead, the Christian dead, what shall he do?

When he stands out there by the grave and faces the tears of the heartbroken (for always we weep as though death were some new and unexpected thing), when these tears moisten the clods of the coffin lid (as no rain from heaven can ever moisten them), will this minister say to those bereaved who wait with repressed emotion to hear him—will he say:

"My friends, Jesus Christ will never again come to this world. It is true he promised he would, but he will not. He did not rise from the dead, his own body long ago yielded to corruption and turned to dust. The body of your dead will never rise from the clutch of death, from the claim of the grave, science, philosophy and historic evidence are all against it; but, for myself, I believe in the 'persistence of personality through death' (p. 98). I would comfort you therefore with this individual opinion of mine."

How like a shameful farce it would be.

What a throwing down of God's Christ and his promise of intended comfort into the mire of the rankest unbelief that ever could exude from a human heart.

And yet this is what the honesty of every man who believes what Dr. Fosdick teaches about the resurrection and the Coming of Christ puts him under bonds to say.

The Effect of Modernism

What shall be said of the general effect when such lectures as "The Modern Use of the Bible" are delivered, such a book circulated, such a ministry as expressed by it welcomed, paraded, exalted and even rapturously applauded by leaders in the Church and exploited by an ever widening zone of professed Christian preachers?

When the man outside, to say nothing of the man in the church and in the pew, hears the modern preacher (the preacher who believes in the modern use of the Bible) deny the Bible doctrine of fiat creation and argue for uniformitarianism, the unbegun, never ending cycles of sameness, birth, death, destruction, recreation and repeated cycles of birth, death, destruction; when he hears the preacher repudiate with much suggested irony the idea of a transcendental God, free and independent of his own creation, at liberty and sufficiently "high powered" to work out his own will, and along the plotted curve of a predestined purpose down to the detail that takes account of the fall of a sparrow and the exact number of the hairs of the head; and then hears him, after this attempted cynicism, talk in flowing phrases of the "immanent" God, at home and at ease in a world where all is well, and knows by the most elemental working of his own mind that this "immanent" God while furnishing a fine adjectival title to con-

jure with before high school graduates and minis-
terial novitiates, in final terms is nothing more
than an impersonal force bound up with, and an in-
tegral part of, the machine, self evolved, and from
which there is no escape; when this listener hears
preachers deny the Bible doctrine of the origin of
man, such as that God formed him by direct action
of His will and power, and hears the preacher
demonstrate that countless ages ago man came up
out of a hint or touch of chlorophyl somewhere in
some far, uncharted sea and then from its unmap-
ped shores with a clinging grain of sand or dust
came through lowest and most repulsive lines of
bestial forms to his present state; when he hears
the preacher deny that sin is treason against the
Most High God, that it is nothing more than con-
genital weakness, physical malformation, lack of
social adjustment; when he hears the preacher
refuse to accept death as the penalty and proof of
sin and witness of the begun judgment of that
God who is carrying all things onward to a final
assize; when he hears him deny there is a hell and
is silent about any promised heaven; when he
hears the modernist preacher say the Bible is
mainly made up of poetry, legendary folk-lore and
miracle narratives that are scientifically and his-

torically "incredible"; that it is some two thousand years verbally out of date and is in absolute conflict with final truth, what can be the conclusion of such a listener, whether saint or sinner, but that the Bible is a book over which no busy, responsible man should spend time either to assail or defend; that at best it is nothing more than a treatise on morals in this life, morals which seem little better practised by those who attempt to defend it than by those who have no interest whatever in it.

What conclusion can a listener to the modern preacher reach about himself, but that Job's question, "If a man die, shall he live again?" has never been answered and that he is absolutely left in the dark about God and his own soul and any "tomorrow" of any sort; and as life is so brief, its tenure so uncertain, and money the only power that counts, his imperative obligation in this swiftly flying present is to lay hold of money, "get rich quick," honestly always, if he can, but, as there is no supreme tribunal before which he must answer in any hereafter, then get rich, seeking only to be quick witted enough to avoid coming into contact with tribunals and judgments here below.

Do you wonder when the advanced preacher repudiates the Bible doctrine of the way of salvation through a penally sacrificial, and blood redeeming Christ, denies a future of eternal woe and personal suffering to those who are "out of Christ," and to all who definitely repudiate him as the Book presents him; do you wonder, not merely at brutal violation of law, but at the uttter deadness to the sense of law; do you wonder at the steadily rising tide of materialism that is drowning out all consciousness of things beyond the length of the eye lashes and the touch of the finger tips?

I am not willing to believe this spirit of worldwide lawlessness that is now abroad is the direct heritage of the recent war.

Nay, rather, I am bound to listen to the old, far question that comes out of this old, old Bible:

"If the foundations be destroyed, what can the righteous do?"

When men who by their profession should stand between the living God and the spiritually dead sinner, men who should cry aloud and spare not, men who should tell the truth about the wrath of God and proclaim the startling proposition, scripturally and intellectually true, that the love of

God has been revealed when and where his wrath was made manifest; when men whose business it is to tell the truth about God, that God can by no means clear the guilty, and that the sinner must meet this God in His redeeming grace or in the judgment that can have no mercy for that unbelief which, had it the power, would banish the Eternal from his throne; when the Ambassador of Christ ceases to preach Christ as the Book commands him to preach, could you expect anything else than the spirit of disintegrating unbelief in the Church and limitless lawlessness in the world?

Modernism Will Fail

But although I have spoken of the danger that lies in such a book as "The Modern Use of the Bible" and the kind of ministry it expresses, I have not the slightest fear in the long run for the faith of God's elect, and rest in the absolute assurance given by the Son of God himself:

"Heaven and earth shall pass away: but my words shall not pass away."

It would not be unedifying to recall all the bold assertions made by infidels in the past as to the ephemeral character of the Book of books, so

many of us still delight to call the "Word of God,"
to recall how their own writings have been put
amid the dust and worm eaten lumber of forgotten
things; how the advance with floating banners in
the name of science, philosophy and new evidence,
self satisfied assurance that the Bible was now to
be overthrown and cast from the place of authority over the mind of man, how that advance
has been turned into a retreat and even a rout,
with the boastful banners trailed in the confession
of defeat, while the ages long and ever living
Book has taken on new authority and won fresh
victory in the realm of faith, and is the demonstration that its words, the simplest and plainest,
are very spirit and very life; so that, in any
library where it is placed upon the shelf it con-
tinues to live when that library turns into a grave-
yard for any decade old book that has set itself
forth in the name and claim of science.

Surely no man will look back upon a world into
which the Gospel came as the fulfilment of the
Old Testament, a Gospel, which, according to
Mark, was "written in the prophets"; no man can
have the hardihood, I am sure, to believe a Gospel
of mere ethics, though it were better, even, than
that of a Seneca or a Marcus Aurelius, a Gospel

that confined its promises to the area of this world
and the life that now is, could have wrought the
change which the story told by Galilean fishermen
as well as by men of Pauline culture has wrought.

An Ethical Christ Not a Saving Christ

So far as mere ethical teaching is concerned,
Jesus Christ himself has given a rebuke that
stands out in definite form on the background of
the ages.

Nicodemus came to him seeking a new doctrine
and looking upon him as the new teacher who
could give him that doctrine.

In a very quiet, yet thoroughly smashing way
Jesus made it plain to this Rabbi that what he
needed was not a **new doctrine,** but a **new life,**
and that he, Jesus himself, so far from being
merely a teacher was no less than the Supreme
Life-giver, he who alone could give that life.

Then he put the way of getting this life before
him in such a manner that there was no room to
misunderstand it.

He told him the familiar story of the people
in the wilderness bitten by serpents, God's
method of delivering them by causing a bit of
brass to be made in the likeness of the serpent

that bit them and nailed to a cross, commanding all who would be saved from death to look at it; and every one that looked lived.

Like that serpent he was to be nailed to a cross, he was to be nailed there in the likeness of the serpent of sin that had bitten people, had bitten people everywhere, bitten them even unto death. God the Father, indeed, would cause him to be nailed there and "made sin."   All those who wanted to escape from death and get a new life that should bring them into saving fellowship with God must believe on him on that cross as God's provided way of salvation.

There were no ethics in that, save the ethics of a new life, a new life to be got from a crucified Son of God who, when risen from the dead, should take his ordained place, not as a remembered teacher, a surviving principle or precept, but as the immortal Life-giver.

It was not an ethical Christ that moved the world over from pagan self-satisfaction, and self blinding philosophy; it was not an ethical Christ that turned the world upside down for the natural man and right side up for God and his Christ and the souls of men.

It is not an ethical Christ that can do that today.

Not an ethical Christ who passed through time and whose vision has been lost on that shore where eternity's waves swallow up all that is only of time.

Not an ethical Christ who passed through the portals of death, leaving behind him only the echo of his unanswered cry, "Why hast thou forsaken me?"

Not an ethical Christ whose preachers preach only "the life that now is," and not a word of "that which is to come."

An ethical Christ may be admired as the world admires a finely chiseled marble statue, but the statue neither produces life nor gives warmth.

Ethics in the name of Christ have been tried on the scale of pretentious systems.

In no garden smitten by winter's frosts are flowers so withered and faded and wholly lifeless as is the Christ who forms the center of such systems.

Nothing so paralyzes as to set before us the work of a Master and bid us copy it.

Shall we seek to copy his sinless life?

How guilty of shameless, bitter mockery is he

who would suggest it.

To live the ethical life!

What is the law of it?

The law is introspection.

Well, when you introspect what are your assets?

How much capital have you to work on?

Introspection—looking within—self analysis!

That is not the law of the Gospel.

The Gospel is just the reverse of that.

Here is the Gospel—listen to it, there is fine music in it.

"Look unto me, and be ye saved."

Look away from yourself.

Look to a Saviour.

Let yourself "be" saved; be the object of salvation—be saved by a Saviour.

That, indeed, is the Gospel.

The thing that moved men, let it be said over and over again, was the most brutal thing that has ever been in the world, that the world has ever looked upon—a Roman cross and a man nailed on it—the Son of God.

The thing that caused that brutal scene to move men was not the mere suffering of the victim, the impulse stirred was neither pity nor compassion.

No.

The moving forces which came out of that blood-red scene was the belief God was there, there in all the majesty of inexorable law, and all the wrath of his essential antagonism to sin; that he was there revealing himself as the God who can by no means clear the guilty, and yet there as the God who in the midst of wrath remembered mercy, the God whose final essence was love, and who sought with all the genius of a God to find a righteous channel for the outflow of his love in saving value to sinful men.

In that cross men saw, not a spasmodic attempt on the part of a crucified man, acting as a martyr in the name of man, seeking to change the mood of God and make him for a passing moment, if not loving, at least, willing to modify his bitterness against man—No! they saw the love of the Son who willingly came out of devotion to the Father that he might provide the righteous channel which God the Father sought for the innate love that yearned over men.   They saw, they were taught to see, not a mere innocent man suffering illegally for guilty men, but the God

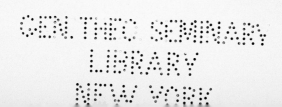

who created a humanity for himself, offering up his humanity that, in the reaction of a righteousness proclaimed, God the Father might still be just and yet the justifier of the ungodly.

That was the Gospel they heard.

It set their constitutional sin natures before them and convinced them that the logic of God's own being required their destruction. Then it revealed to them the immense sweep of God's love in that he himself by a grace that should reign through righteousness had produced a salvation which glorified his law and revealed his love.

What God was for man and what Christ in his blood and his agony translated him to be, moved men, moved them to hate sin that at such a price made it necessary for such a way of salvation, and led them to seek the God who, while he hated sin, loved the sinner.

Think of it!

A God who could not break his law for love's sake, a God who would not break his law for love's sake, and a Son of God who found a way by which the law of God should be honored and become the very channel for divine love to flow forth legally to men.

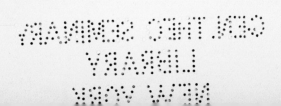

It is a way of salvation that bears the stamp and seal of God from the beginning to the end.

The Gospel Future

This Gospel set a future before men.

Not merely a diaphanous, ghost life that somehow, in some way, should "persist" somewhere, that neither faith nor reason could find anywhere, and, so far as the surveyor's chain went, was nowhere.

Nothing like that nebulousness. They expected, they looked for, something far better than that. They expected him who for us men and our redemption came down to where we were, would come again to finish the redemption he had begun, in giving us the body that in God's original purpose belonged to the soul, and without which this announced purpose of God would be an open failure.

They were taught to believe God is now, in this age, creating a spiritual race of sons of God, that these sons, spiritually, are yet in the embryo state, that at the last and in logical consequence of his return this race would be completed, a race of immortal, God-like men, to

dwell on the earth as their ordained abode and
to dwell in it forever.

Such a Gospel as that has no fear of any demol-
ishable "framework" in its construction, it is
strong enough, spiritual enough, loyal and divine
enough to hold itself intact against any wind of
doctrine or philosophy that may blow.

The Need of the Church

What the Church needs now is to return to that
Gospel.

If there is any withering in the Church today
it is because of the Christ of mere ethics so in-
tensively preached to men, the Christ who never
reaches the cross as the Saviour of men, the
Christ who never rose from the dead, the Christ
who instead of calling us to look away from self
and look unto him as the victor over sin and death
and the grave, bids us look within and apply his
earthly precepts and principles, his "ideals" (God
forgive me for even quoting that dishonoring,
cheapening, leveling concept; think of it, the
"ideals" of Christ, just as though he were a mere
man among men comparing his ideas with theirs,
his "ideals" with theirs!)—bids us so incorporate

his ethics that they may arouse the birth right divinity in us, and said to be, like his.

If there is any trembling, any oscillating, any rocking to and fro that seemingly threatens the stability of the Church as though the very foundations were crumbling, it is because of the too willing Uzzahs who seek to steady the ark with their modernistic hands.

The ark was in peril from the first, not because the oxen stumbled, but because neither the oxen nor the new cart had any right of relation to the ark at all.

When the cart and oxen were substituted for the shoulders of the sons of Kohath the trouble and the peril began.

When David undertook to bring the ark to Jerusalem in his way and not in God's way the disaster was ordained and there was no escape from it. The substitution of man's way and man's concept for God's way and God's concept in the Church and particularly in the pulpit in the proclamation of a Gospel that is not the Gospel, carries with it the assurance of the judgment of God.

The need of the Church is to go according to

God's mind and God's way as set forth in the Scriptures committed to her keeping.

The Church does not need the Uzzahs of "agreed" scholarship who would steady the Church as she faces the science and philosophy of the hour.

The Church does not need men to stand forth and apologize for her "framework," or reorganize her thought forms so that they may come more fully into agreement with man's mind and man's thought.

To discard the First century for the sake of the Twentieth and make the Church and the Bible conform to that is just of the same wisdom that would discard the foundation of a house for the sake of the roof.

Over against all attempt at repair, reorganization or would-be apology for the Church in her constitution, her Gospel, and the claimed necessity of swinging into line with the march of the twentieth century toward naturalism under the plea of a larger and freer consciousness of God in the soul, a consciousness that will deliver the individual in the Church from dependence on mere verbalism and deliver the Church from being hampered and held and made static and frozen into lifeless form by mere words whose content fall short of the actual revelation of God in the soul today; over against all this setting up of the will of man instead of the revealed and dynamically demonstrated will of God revealed in the first century in a text form charged with all the vitality of the limitless spirit of God, able to thrill and surge through the soul in consciousness of God with apocalyptic power; over against all this attempt of modernism, there is the immense declaration of that Scripture which defines the Church for the last century as it does for the first:

"The house of God, which is the church of the living God, the pillar and ground of the truth" (I Tim. 3:15).

It seems in reality a pitiful thing that any man calling himself an ambassador of the God who created and united to himself the humanity in which to meet the demand of his own being against the wilfulness of the sinner he would save, it seems pitiful when the ambassador of such a God is willing to go forth and apologize for that Bible which underwrites the Church and underwrites the commission of the ambassador and is in itself a witness of the creating and ordaining hand of God, as much a witness as the Orion and

Pleiades he upholds or the cross he foresaw and whereon he become the omnipotent Saviour of man.

It is not necessary to defend the Bible, to go out and call in the scientist, the philosopher and the historian whose knowledge, with all the advance that has been made, is still in the nebulous and suggestive, rather than the final and static, state.

It is not necessary to defend the Bible and prove that the God who hangs the earth on nothing, sent horses and chariots of fire to take Elijah to Heaven, horses and chariots of fire which he himself defines as the colorful and manifold glory of the angels which even the most materialistic unbeliever is not in position evidentially to deny. It is not necessary to go out and seek witnesses to prove an iron axe head can swim in water as easily (when necessary) even as a machine heavier than air can rise any day above the clouds and float there as a swan upon the bosom of a placid lake; or, that by an X-ray we may tell (as the Psalmist announced three thousand years ago) all our bones; or, that it is easy now to send a whisper round the globe, and that men on the other side of the sea may be justified or condemned by their words which we hear on this farther shore; or, that out of the viewless air we may receive both the words and the pictured face and form of those we love beyond our sight in a distant land, with the wide sea spread between. This and much more, for believing which, fifty years ago, science and arrogant philosophy and much fuss making historic evidence would have arrested all such persons and put them in the pillory of intellectual contempt.

No! It is not necessary to go out and call in the mediocre witness of limited human understanding, limited more or less by the age in which it lives, to prove the truth of this Bible that overtops the times and with calm, unruffled voice tells the facts of history future with the same certitude as history past.

I repeat it is not necessary to defend the Bible.

Of all things on earth it needs least to be defended, demonstrated or proved.

The Bible carries its own defense.

It is fully armed and equipped at every point. The defense of the Bible is the Bible itself.

What is needed in the Church in this hour is men who will preach the Bible, preach it faithfully, fully, never altering an original word, nor carrying it around the corner or through a short cut from the main route.

What is needed in the Church is that the preacher shall preach it as the infallible Word of God, preach it and not parley about it.

It is not the unbelief of the world that is hindering the acceptance of the Bible.

It is not the new evidence, the new knowledge, the new findings of science, none of these things is making it difficult for the world and the intelligence of the world to accept it.

Not at all!

The talk about a new world needing a new Bible or a new interpretation that shall make a new Bible out of the Old is at best but unspiritual, as it is, also, unintellectual, chatter.

Why Talk about a New World Needing a New Bible?

Where is this new world needing a new Bible? What is so new in it?

It is a question that is coming up on the lips of men.

I repeat the question and I ask myself, What is so new in the world?

Children are still born at the risk of a mother's
life.

In spite of every invention disease still outruns
the last edition of Materia Medica.

The surgeon's knife still finds, not only the old
gangrene deep seated in the flesh, but deeper still,
the old sin, the old shame and the incurable re-
morse.

What is there new?

Men still laugh, and swear to hide a groan.

Pleasure still fills the cup to the brim and then
leaves the dregs of old weariness and the deep
disgust of sated lust at the bottom of the cup.

What, really, is new?

Men still struggle against inherited appetite
and passions, are possessed by them as by very
demons and at last are dragged down by them
into the whelming misery of moral helplessness
and despair.

Talk about building a new world?

Why, the old acquaintances meet you at every
turn, in the same old clothes, in the same old
fashion, doing the same old things, and doing
them in the same old way.

The old acquaintances—the familiar forms.

There they are—sin, shame, red-faced and

never satisfied lust, hungry greed, slimy, serpent
like falsehood, the cowardly, crawling, innuendo,
the faint praise that damns while it praises, brute
selfishness that would sacrifice the dearest love,
the thirst for gain that will drink at every foun-
tain fair or foul.

A new world, you say, needing a new Bible, a
Bible fitted to a new world?

Why deceive yourself?

The old cannon, the old bombs, the old torch
are all here and the old war is harnessing itself
for a fresh welter of blood that it may revel
in it as it has done ever since the impassable sky
looked down on the first murder nearer to God's
environment by some thousands of years than
now and upon the first war inspired by the same
wild beast that still lurks in the lair of the same
old human heart.

No! I say it is not a new world demanding a
new Bible, rather it is an old world needing an
old, old Bible.

The Opposition to the Bible is Not
from the World

The opposition and hindrance to the Bible, I
assure you, do not come from the world. It is not

the world out there throwing stones at the Bible and seeking to stifle its full message.   There is doubt out there and sorrow and perplexity and natural unbelief, but there is no organized effort to throw the Bible down into a discount of open contempt.   Instead of that there is a willingness to listen to any comfort the Bible can bring, to any relief to the ulcer on the shoulder where the burden rubs the hardest.

The hindrance and the opposition come from an entirely different direction.

They come from the theological seminary, the theological seminary whose professors have forgotten (if they ever knew) how to read the old Bible, and read it in the old way.

They come from the pulpit, pulpits that proclaim themselves modern and new.   It is the unbelief of the professor and the preacher, tempted to play the role of the prophet to a so-called new age.

It is a profound mistake to think such an attitude is intellectual.

It is not particularly so.

The most intellectual, as it is the most honest and the most loyal, attitude for the Christian minister, is to submit his mind to the Bible (if he undertakes to preach it at all) as the written

Word of God, and take it as it comes to him, in the assurance, if he will compare Scripture with Scripture (not with science and new philosophy) he shall see light in God's light, and be able to give it undimmed to others.

Let the preacher preach the Bible as the Word of God and the Blood of Christ as that chemistry of infinite love by which, though sins "be as scarlet, they shall be as white as snow; though they be red like crimson, they shall be as wool."

The Great Opportunity

There never was an hour when a greater opportunity was offered to a preacher to take this undying Book, expound it, expose its content, reveal its beauty, stir the mind of men with its matchless wonders, fill the soul with its Heaven bequeathed peace, let its music play upon the heart chords, let the grip of its power hold men back from the edge of the downward plunge, and by the gentleness of its touch lead the spirit up to illumined heights, let it paint the glories of the delectable mountains, show the Way that leads to the opened gates, to the city and the throne, and where he sits bearing the marks of the wounds he got for the sake of sinful men, allow it to demonstrate itself to the intellect, the conscience and the heart.

In their strange demand for liberty to think independently of any textual or ritual trammels, preachers fail to search the Book for itself and thus discover the liberty of the Spirit, the real freedom which is willing and glad, "not to think above that which is written."

It is evident enough that no self-respecting man would be willing to prove his statement true to him who should rudely, violently, take him by the throat and demand it; rather, he would resent such violence and keep his secret.

When men come to the Bible with the speech of suspicion and accusation on their lips and rank and cynical unbelief in the heart and clutch it in the grip of a defiance that says: "Prove to us you are telling the truth, prove it by the standards we set up for you," could you expect it to do anything else than to keep its silence and withhold the illumination it otherwise is ready to give?

What an opportunity then to stand forth, take the Book at its own value, and wait for the result.

He who stands, holds in his hand and discusses

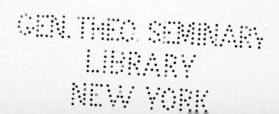

the quality and value of a seed while summer days are passing and the inviting soil still waits to receive it, is not wise; but wise is he who casts in the seed and finds in quick result the truth of all its claims.

Let the preacher preach the Bible with the unshaken conviction that it is the very Word of God, the message from himself; let him preach it faithfully, insistently, above all the noise of contending hours, and he will see the same result as all the passing centuries have revealed, the calling out of the elect and chosen ones in whom faith is the gift of God and in whose soul the fruitage of the Book will make manifest that it is, indeed, as the Apostle with challenging note has said, "Not the word of men, but in truth, the word of God;" that Word of God which still gives its unmodified command to every true ambassador of Christ:

"Study to shew thyself approved unto God, a workman that needeth not to be ashamed, rightly dividing the word of truth" (II Tim. 2:15).

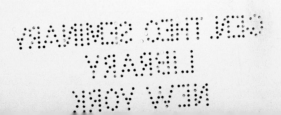